Deenewood

Deenewood

A Sequence

Arlene Swift Jones

Turning Point

Published by Turning Point
P.O. Box 541106
Cincinnati, OH 45254-1106

ISBN: 1932339167
LCCN: 2003109424

Poetry Editor: Kevin Walzer
Business Editor: Lori Jareo

Typeset in Transition 521 by WordTech Communications LLC,
Cincinnati, OH

Visit us on the web at www.turningpointbooks.com

"First Winter of Sarah Thomas Schwartz' Unmarked Grave" first
appeared in *Green Mountains Review*.

Cover photo by Robert Aranow.

Contents

1. *John Williams Thomas*   *1842–1914*

    m. Jennie Humphrey, 1883   *1860–1885*

2. *John Williams Thomas, II*   *1885–1948*

    m. Lucy Wheelock, 1914   *1895–1968*

3. *Sarah Thomas*   *1920–1983*

    m. David Schwartz, 1943   *1920–1989*

3. *John Williams Thomas, III*   *1922–*

    m. Andrea McNeill (speaker), 1953   *1930–*

1. 1990

Thomas' Estate Auction

(Andrea, speaker)

The gavel sounds upon the auction block

for an 18th century Chinese-porcelain:

a woman warrior sits astride a dragon

each minutely scrolled in red and gold,

a thread of blue. Once upon a time her sword

was broken—it is badly mended, "but expertly

repaired will be invisible," barks the auctioneer....

Invisible as the heart, I think, beneath

the hard gilt folds of her kimono, and,

like the dragon's rounded belly—a *piñata*—

stored with hidden, witnessed sorrows

(daughters once rounded mine with joy).

On what new mantlepiece or pedestal

will she be enshrined to watch the years

accumulate, take shape like galaxies;

or fall down on the hearth and both be broken.

The bronze team of horses, by Fremiet,

now stand, in harness and hard sheepskin saddles—

their ears attentive to each other only,

deafened to the hum of buyers—

straining equally in a non-ending pull.

The nuzzle of one upon the other honors them,

bronze or flesh: I would stand, forever,

within their ken. I feel their hard

endurance rising in my throat...Going! going!

But *I* am gone, and leaving, pass downstairs

through the stable, where the scent of horse

is only dust on dust, as faint as horse smell

on the bronzes. In the stable attic a rusted sleigh

and carriage slept one hundred years and never

will awaken, their upholstery

inhabited by mice that burrow there,

and have for generations.

                            Like the dragon lady—

endless stories of the dead are locked inside me,

but mine are fighting to be free. For now I 'll sit

among the living, my back against the high-backed

boulder reflected in the pond and try

not to think of yesterday, or of tomorrow

and to forget today. I'll watch the trees

move upside down reflected in the glassy water.

What winter yet to come will further separate

the stones I sit on, what weather ease them down

into the muddy edge?

                            I hear the bric-a-brac

dispensed, and know each piece: the coral piglets'

squeal, an ivory elephant still looking

for his lost proboscis, quite broken off

as long as I remember. "Late 18th century carving,"

quotes the auctioneer, "but you need high ceilings..."

I know those high carved walnut beds, married

with mahogany, where death and love

were consummated, the passions of so many spent.

I watch the wild goose glide on the pond's dark water

in a vigil for his nesting mate.

His arched black neck, white cheeks are mirrored

in smoky glass; I see her head above the grasses

on the island like a lily on its pad.

How patiently she sits, she waits,

while the distant drone of loss accumulates

of what I never wanted until I see it go.

I'd rather *be* the dragon lady, sentience frozen,

desire inarticulate; or be the wild goose

with an instinct only for tomorrow.

I'm not the son or even daughter

of this house cracked open like an oyster,

what was thought to be its pearls

strewn and peered at by every public eye.

I watch the infant green of budding willow,

black hemlocks like bronzed eagles

swooping, the sun-drenched green of maples,

pyramids of opening horse-chestnut flowers—

all together mottled shadows sweeping

over water, over lawns where bright moss

thins and thickens. A bullfrog hrumphs and bellows,

a trout leaps for mayflies, sends concentric rings

across the hemisphere of pond, confining

them between the wall and bank.

Sit beside me, love of yesterday...

Watch with me. See how we are bedded

in the walls, the grass, the moss; see

our faces ripple in the water, grinning

back at us in ever bigger circles.

Keep your back—like mine—hunched against

the voices that we hear, how they clamor

for the things held dear enough, it seemed,

the saving of consumed so many lives.

For I would rather not be here, nor you,

to hear the insistent barking coinage

of the auctioneer.

2. 1955

The Clock's Chime

(Andrea, speaker)

In my sleep three initials, scrolled

on linen, cover me. They are engraved

on silver forks and spoons, knives, gilded

on cups and dinner plates, *to remind me*

who I am, lest I forget. The travel clock

is now a mantel clock: peacocks scrolled

in bronze are caged inside glass walls. It struck

the hour to watch the brave Six Hundred.

Now that clock counts out the minutes of my life.

Will they stagger, like a water drop

not wanting to let go, but falling? I touch

the button of the clock to strike the hour.

Have I, too, become the keeper

of useless documents, seals of blistered

red, housed in a metal storage box?

I watch the papers crumble, half-wanting them

to stay....Cairo's *Hotel Shepheard* stickers

peel from a leather trunk which slumps

beneath the mantle, holding sticks of kindling.

How they bruise and scar the satin lining

that was green.

                  Two pink coral pigs

and an ivory elephant battle where they stand

in a polished glaze of a tilt-top pie crust table.

Maybe in the tilt, once, those bloodless

wounds occurred: chipped snouts, snapped-off lower

trunk, one foot hacked to an incisor's point

on the two-inch pachyderm.

                    An ivory box:

a monkey floats on a coral branch, petals

breached; one hand grasps the hole of the gone

inlay, there are empty eyes in his kimono.

Coral butterflies, fixed in never-rising

flight, and a ladybug, still black and red,

watch a pale praying mantis. I lift

the top to find inside a braided ring

of burnished hair, a yellowed note:

A *token of our promises. Your Jenny.*

3. 1979

To John Williams Thomas

(Andrea, speaker)

Riding above a roll top desk

is an engraving, inscribed to you:

> "To JWT, *with kind regards,*
>
> *the Countess of Cardigan, 1892,*
>
> *at Deene, the Seat of Cardigan in Wales*":

I try to piece together puzzles of your life

    unknown to us who live within your shadow,

        your bric-a-brac, mementos, in *your* house

            you, with Lord Cardigan's high-bred nose,

                his noble expectations.

            Saber aloft, he rides and rides his charger, Ronald,

        on your paneled study wall, engraved from

ancestral portraits that climb up sweeping stairs

in Deene's White Hall (below those costumed poses

are Ronald's hoof and Ronald's head, stuffed

and mounted under glass). Generations

of this house have honored Cardigan's famous

charge at Balaclava: how *he* led

six hundred seventy-three (*you* recorded it)

gray-jacketed dragoons, scarlet-tunicked lancers

11th Hussars in cherry-pink trousers

by Cardigan's Bond Street glory-smitten tailors

who cheered them off to war.

Prince Albert and the Queen stepped out

at Buckingham and the Queen said *There there*

to the eager Prince of Wales, 12 years old.

Someday you too, my son... the crowd was crazed

with pride of England, *Keep your pecker up,*

old boy, never say die, they shouted to see

such unspared splendor of nobility

and rank so brilliantly got up for war,

such sabers, brass enough on rows

of marching chests to feed a cannon's forge.

You must have loved it all, the Queen, the great hurrahs

for war, *noblesse oblige*, the tiers of seats you sat in,

under parasols, on Telegraph Hill with the gentry

of Sevastopol, mother-of-pearl opera glasses

readied to watch 673 men glitter

like birds of paradise. You must have been there—

were you there? It was a sunny day.

The first line of 300 mounted men,

their weapons lances mounted on bamboo,

or sabers, attacked a line of waiting Russian

cannon on the hill. Viewers saw red

tongues hiss, then spew out cannon balls,

heard horses' screams above the deafening boom.

They saw Sergeant Talbot, headless, reins

clutched, sword arm still aloft, ride on

for 40 yards. In twenty minutes, only

30 of 600 horsemen were alive.

Then Lord Cardigan, on Ronald, leapt

a Russian gun, in his plumed fur shako hat—

all agreed he looked magnificent. Stunned viewers saw the gunners

flee.   You saw the best of men fight bravely on a pleasant day

before the smoke of cannon crept up hills

with regimental tents like distant dragon's teeth

that wouldn't spring to life, or be awakened.

Limbs and heads, sodden uniforms

of lancers, hussars and dragoons

and broken hooves of horses sowed the valley.

4. 1960

World War II Veteran

(Andrea, speaker)

At night in bed

he kicks the enemy

(but I am there).

He strikes the air

with a fist, muttering

words without softness.

His dreams are metal,

steel blue and unyielding,

nothing exquisite. No

children sleeping,

no comfort of apples.

Who comes to him

in the night, and lays hands

upon him, maiming

what it didn't kill?

5. 1935

Lucy Wheelock Thomas

(speaker)

I entered Deenewood holding my bouquet

white as my wedding gown. I saw the lilies

fade, I smelled their sweet decay

in that dark hall, dimmed by leaded windows.

What light remained was blocked by rusty velvet

draperies—once, I think they were blood-red.

But eyes adjust to darkness...Outside

snow lay bright on top the ground.

The wallpaper reached out, entangling me

with leaves of grey and brown, blue

outlined in black, that twined and climbed

the walls, up two open stairways.

As I stopped on the stairs, I saw

initials frosted on the leaded glass:

JWT. I didn't know I would

become their *gardienne,*

It was 1914, and I, the first wife

at *Deenewood.* I served tea to guests,

cucumber sandwiches and *petit fours*

at four o'clock, on Limoges china. Dinner

was refined—candles, subdued conversation

that began with soup and went through courses.

After Archduke Ferdinand's assassination

in Sarajevo and the Kaiser's vow

to stand by Austria, my husband had nothing

more to say to me: he went to war.

Sarah arrived

when he was gone. He came back, with less

to say. Then I was lucky—I had a son

to keep the male initials that monogrammed

the house. My own, in curliques—

on a dozen silver goblets—lay

in a hard silk-covered box with anti-tarnish

lining. Such things, increasingly unused,

I locked in closets.

                    I could not love

this house, so I possessed it, fiercely—*with*

its *objets*—to guard it for my son. I knew

it was a house most girls would dream of. I talked

to Jennie, who watched from picture frames; I touched

her name—gilt letters tooled on her Bible.

She should have been a playmate, together

we should have tried on our wedding dresses

in the attic (Hopelessly, I wanted

her approval).

I tried to isolate my children from anger

in the house—it spewed like foam sputtering

from the brook's swollen flow in spring,

when rotted leaves choke passages. I bit

my tongue bloody holding anger back,

asking Jenny to *admire* (again talking

to a photo) and then to calm

her raging son, while from the clock I'd wound

and polished, I heard the peacocks cry.

When my son was sent away

to boarding school, I broke every rule

with my daughter: we smoked in stealth,

I stole my husband's cigarettes....

                              What

is there for you, my daughter, but to marry?

Yet emptiness will be what you embrace.

And what for you, my son? Don't come back

till you can claim what will be yours—what I

have kept for you. And never bring a bride

where she's not welcome.

6. 1955

John Williams Thomas

(speaker)

Daughter, what did you do? What *did* you do?

You married a Jew! A Jew! You had four sons,

each one of them a Jew! You erased my line,

you with your bloody Jew. I could have had

a future lineage if you'd been the son.

Damn you, to marry a Jew!

Your brother was not meat for me.

Adored by his mother she sent him off

to boarding school to get away from me.

Half of him resembled me—but his sad eyes!

My God! how they reminded me of failure:

of my own, of my marriage to a woman

bred to serve a man. But I was used to servants.

What else was there for her, for any woman,

but to serve a man? And I was a catch.

I learned to hate how she countenanced me.

I hated me. But then...No! I did not. Any woman

I admired must stand up to me

and *she* did not. She wilted like a flower

in drought. Who got the best of whom—of her,

or me?

How could I have loved a daughter more

than I could love a son? You stood up to me,

in fear at first, and then contempt.

My mother-wilted son I could not admire

any more than I admired myself.

His eyes reflected back the sorrow

that was my own: my stern-faced father

giving daily homage to a woman

I had never known and learned to hate—

his bride, a phantom mother. I thought

that boys with mothers were in storybooks.

Though he never told me, I could see

the way he looked at me he saw his love

awry, he saw her die, and knew himself

and I death's instruments....

Daughter, I said the *world's* awry

when one dines daily with a *presence,*

ghostly for me, lingering in a house,

and sees his father stand and stare at space,

half-expecting, hoping *she* might fleetingly

appear, that he, somehow, could undo

his appetites and she could love him still.

I swore I could not live as he lived. I

have not!

       Children are not made

in heaven. Can one desire a woman

never taught to love, but taught to *bear it?*

Daughter, I could not! My *ladies*

were not ladies, but they served a purpose

well, for which they were intended.

Sex was not, to them, a burden.

You have borne it! But in spite of me,

in order to erase my tree with Jews

for sons. They are not my grandsons

and I...I have done with you.

7. 1980

Lucy's Letter Opener

(Andrea, speaker)

This ivory Chinese letter opener clearly has been

here for ages, in the living room's desk drawer,

a desk become a table by its disuse—

except to put things on.

The carved handle tells a story, in relief:

three figures climb the handle; the first

sits on an inward curve, in dismay looks up

at him who seems fixed firmly in the air

and who gestures to the third—a woman—standing

in a balcony-pagoda. He smiles,

one arm akimbo (nose to knee, the first man

stoops and pleads): the other raised to her.

His hair becomes the trunks of supple trees

with flowers at the top and over

the pagoda. His face is cheerful

but hers is worn—effaced—by opening letters

from that distant sea, when grandfather went

to China, Malaysia, India, and Japan,

judging from the stamps that someone saved.

And from the *objets* sent to her, who stayed.

8. 1965

John Williams Thomas, III

(John Williams Thomas, speaker)

The same year that Grandfather was buried

by the fenced-in boulder on the hill

my father married. His bride came to a house

that had never known a wife:

Jenny stood framed on the roll-top desk,

and peered, in miniature, from every bedside

table. From every room, she seemed to watch

my Mother, as we became another

generation of a son and daughter:

we learned to move tight-lipped.

         The fence grew higher

as my father's face grew fixed. He screamed

with gout. Morphine made him quiet, a habit

he acquired as easily as rain falls

in a season of monsoon. The house

endured as best it could: mother and daughter

linked together, smoking in the attic.

I grew a tight knot in my chest.

Daddy threw me in the water, teaching

me, he thought, to swim; he placed me—

my first time—on a pony, then smacked him hard.

But I fell off and he called me incompetent;

he thought it was disgraceful to have such

a son, when I lay bleeding. He put me back

to try the whole thing over. He believed

necessity should be my teacher.

Though now no portrait of him hangs on any

wall, I fear the mirror: I can't erase

his face from mine, nor tear his glares,

like wind-whipped dust, from out from the corners

of my eyes. His lower lip extends,

just slightly, ready to expel his anger;

his eyes are hard, like coal. They never looked

at me, except to pare me down to half

my size—and I was small. Still small, he sent

me off to boarding school: *Mothers*, he said,

should never raise their sons! They are only

brood mares. And daughters never matter.

His mementos? I want to burn them all,

but something stops me: I want to prove

him wrong, how—like girls' souvenirs

of beaus and signed-for dances—he kept ball

invitations in a thick scrapbook,

ticket stubs for college games and theater,

French menus, with several kinds of oysters;

lists of ships' passengers (he under-

lined his name), seating charts for the captain's

table with doodles of his own initials.

His *documents?* Unlike his father, no official seals

in trunks, no invitations for a visit

to the queen. Only letters that

he wrote to women, who sent them back addressed

to Mother (which she never threw away.

I found them in a shoe-box in her closet

tied with string). His final record—his grave

left nameless by my mother.

                            Both names in bronze—

my mother's and my father's—I bolted

on the boulder (beneath *his* father's),

but separately, as they were in life.

I buried their ashes, leaving space enough

between so they would never touch.

There still is space upon the boulder

for generations. But alas! I have no sons.

9. 1965

From a Daughter-in-law, to Lucy

(Andrea, speaker)

Did I store the darkness of this house

inside of me and did it pass, like genes,

into my daughters? Will their blood tell?

In my blank unknowing did I wish

they had been sons?

                    Lucy, when Kari came

you said A *third child of my son yet still*

a daughter! Silence cloaked us like a pall.

But, once my belly rounded with a son,

you thought that I'd withheld before, that I

had chosen to deny your son's—and your—

own heart's desire. When my son withered

in my body, rejecting life, rejecting

me—when he came limping into the world

before his time and he was dead, you said

and only to me, *Spite has no dimensions—*

it is as endless as the ocean. But,

to your son you spoke of my grief, and

your love for me.

                    Lucy, you possess

your son as you possess this house, with every

objet. We breathe air that you don't want

disturbed—my three daughters and your four *Jew*-grandsons.

Seven grandchildren! We tiptoe among your ghosts,

not one a Thomas boy to carry on

the name you cling to.

    Lucy, you never knew

that I was glad my son was dead.

Don't touch! Don't touch! is written everywhere.

Don't use this spoon, this pot to make castles

in the sand, for frogs. Don't slam doors.

No playing in the house. No crying.

                                        Above

the tangled sounds of summer—cicadas singing

in the afternoon, the rush of falling

water—once I heard a sobbing from

the silent house. I found Kari hiding

in a closet, her tears unstoppable,

her body heaving so she couldn't speak.

Was it your shoe's anger that kicked her, Lucy?

It could not be *you*, awakened from

a nap by a child that went to pee

and flushed a toilet, your son's last child *and* daughter.

10. 1975

Wicker

(Andrea, Speaker)

In May the long verandah stirs and stretches.

All winter long painted chairs

and sofas wait—such cold white stares—

the spider-web wicker frozen in the

love seat thaws and the spiders climb—

a lacy ascension. Doors open, trapped

air whispers through screened windows, pushing

long-backed sturdy rockers to a ghostly

rocking.

        Winter-whitened plants return

to the verandah: from its pot the cream-

edged ivy reaches down a wrought-iron

stand that blooms with hard black iron rosebuds.

Rusted metal tendrils curl, grab

cascading ivy. A stuffed alligator

casts a glassy eye at flintstone arrows,

native spears from Africa, poised

next to scaly dragons, coiled on a parked

buffet.

I recline on a Victorian couch

in a forgotten corner; the sun has bleached

once-scarlet silky tassels on its scrolled headrest

to mud. The bronze bear family with two cubs

holds the open door, four noses press

against glass panes, sniffing pale shells

in a Wedgewood bowl—the shells are longing

for the sea.

       Plums and peaches sit,

rigid, on a Limoges thistle plate,

with three stiff, fooled flies in a dusty

circle—the fruit inedible, the scent

of marble cold.

But something is alive

here: four lions roar on a Morris chair,

camels and the sphinx step out, in sepia,

from stereoscopic views into the green

of laurel, jaded spruce and oak, old

blooming ivy on the chimney. Here

the Holy Land's alive, sun-baked and glaring

out through cobwebbed windows.

11. 1975

To John Williams Thomas, III

(Andrea, Speaker)

My poor maimed one, my bridegroom of long ago...

All John Williams Thomases, except for you,

are only photos on the paneled study wall

where Cardigan still rides. John Williams

was found alive among the dead at Antietam.

His son, your father, served at Ypres. He came

back silent and white-lipped. You, once

a brass-buttoned boy cadet, couldn't wait

to wear tight-waisted trousers and those hard,

plumed hats. You commanded Chrysler horses

in 1944, dueling Krupp

in a tank you nicknamed Ronald. Your young CO

was standing next to you when his head was split

in two. You took command and took the town,

then went to Cardiff on a stretcher, cheered

by half the town with your same name, you—

the oldest wounded officer at twenty-one...

    And then the war was over:

bluebirds flew at Dover.

After that where else but home to those

same *objets*, bric-a-brac you didn't want

to own but must possess, handed down

in one straight line and yours, you feared,

was ending.

            You added medals to the study:

a Purple Heart, a Silver Star

for extraordinary bravery. A nervous tic

was added to the left side of your face

(I'd never know, you said, of dangers

you had passed).

            You brought home a swastika

blazing on a banner that had spanned

that Nazi town. You said the stains

were Nazi blood—different from your own,

but not worse than your father's

I think you said. But he was dead.

12. 1967

To My Daughter-in-law, from Lucy

(Lucy, speaker)

You were the second wife to come to Deenewood,

but one was there before who never left—

she will be with you still. I never knew

if she watched *over* me or *watched* me,

or ever knew if she approved of me.

Her son did not. I had, I thought, the season's

match. When my dream house palled, I sickened,

but I didn't die.

       You could not know

of battles that I fought, the ways I went

to guard my son and daughter. When you came

I wondered how you could be worth what I

had paid. Perhaps I made you pay for that.

Maybe I became your albatross

as *he,* and *she,* were mine. I do not ask

forgiveness. But, you took the fruits

of my endeavors, *you,* and left no heir

for him—you left him daughters. I can say

that they are beautiful, and beauty has

some merit: maybe they'll redeem him still,

and marry well.

              Not knowing, how can I leave

what I tended carefully as a shepherd

guards his flock, his lambs? *My* lamb!

But I give you this…brought to me

by my father from the East, this emerald,

ringed with diamonds. I have gazed at it,

watched its cool fire flicker

in an aureole of starry light.

When I was in the darkest of my days,

I found light here, that is dimming now

for me, this greeny fire, and will go out.

13. 1968

Sarah Thomas Schwartz

(Sarah, speaker)

You can't see it ahead, ever, only

the years behind we can't undo.

You were alone, Mother, and lonely, too:

we both warred with my father.

What enemy did he fight—his wasted life?

But his last battlefield was where we stood.

I'm glad he suffered pain for he deserved it,

though it wracked us too. I would not

have done for him what I now do for you.

Mother, you lie propped-up, glass-eyed

and staring, your mouth askew, but not with words—

they're gone from you forever. Mute Mother,

once you had a girlish voice, with laughter

that froze to silence when you entered father's house—

his father's house. I remember, still, your voice

when it returned to you, some time after father

screamed at us—he blamed us for his dying...

I thought you would be free but it was too late:

you had become, already, *la concierge.*

For years you unwrapped and polished, then wrapped up

the silver, glued back the browning roses

and darkening monochrome of leaves on walls—

the paper that had loosened, wanting to be free.

You battled moths for ownership of clothes:

you said they'd visited the queen

and showed me photos. You tied and retied letters

in a bundle. I have never read them:

now I will. Maybe I'll find out

how love can come and go.

I remember when your voice stopped altogether,

the day you fell half-paralyzed but knowing—
I saw the knowing in your eyes, I found you
sprawled upon the floor.

                               I too, Mother,
may expect it—something that you gave me
in my blood, your XX chromosomes
bequeathed to me. Mother, listen,
can you hear me? Can you understand
how you made leftovers into life for me
(sometimes I hated how you cringed
but didn't cry). There will be, perhaps,
no one to do for me what I now do for you.

Forgive me, Mother, but I know you'd
bless me, though blessings never came
to our house. But with this, I bless you.
See my gloved hand, Mother. It looks
so lady-like and innocent. The nurses smiled

when they let me in, seeing a dutiful,

loving daughter, in soft suede gloves,

matching black suede shoes—you liked to see me

dressed properly: *It never hurts to see*

a lady dressed like a lady, I hear you say.

I dressed in black today for you.

Today you are *my* daughter,

you are Persephone in late season

and I Demeter, who will stay to mourn.

Mother, see how gently now I touch you,

flex my thumb and finger

and through my glove a lethal serpent stings.

You'll soon be drawn away

by coal black and fiery horses

but I must leave, composed, who am dry-eyed

with fear, although I never believed

that anything I've ever done was right

'til now: *Mother, I've done it all alone!*

Dear Mother, Bless me!

14. 1970

David Schwartz

(David, speaker)

Did she love *me*, or love defiance of her father more?

I loved *her* for herself, her name—so unadorned.

Purity descended of its own on such a name.

Her father said my name would bruise her heel,

wherever her foot would fall.

He said my seed was stones her womb

would shelter or *not* shelter

if he had anything to say, and he had plenty.

I thought to be American was to be chosen.

My Russian father was driven from his village

by a pogrom he swore

his son would never see.

I went to New York's Latin School.

What it was like to be a Jew in Russia

my father kept from me. I never was

a Jew that way until I could not step my foot

upon *her* father's hill—he called it *Thomas Mountain*.

Defying him, she married me, unwelcome

stranger in the house he fled for half a day,

her mother grieving to attend. There were

no friends invited. She walked down the open stair

on her brother's arm. You'd have thought,

except for him, the marriage was a funeral.

He was so full of high and noble expectations

of the war, and said, "I'm off tomorrow."

It was '44. For their mother it was a day

she'd lose both son and daughter.

I stood there

by the stone hearth on a winter April day

repeating words I meant with all my heart—

I loved her even more for the courage

I knew she had to marry me.

                    But

all these years I never knew how much

—or *if*—she loved me. She never said and I,

I wouldn't ask: in the musty air

of Deenewood, as though in stone, it's written that blood

can keep no secrets. Her father said her blood

would someday tell: the names she gave our sons

were *her* family's names after *her* blood

but they are Schwartzes!

                    At Sunday summer dinners—

Lucy and her son presided—we were

twelve, six Schwartzes and six Thomases.

Once—I don't remember what it was

that I had said—John's voice shattered me:

Mr. Schwartz, I said Shut Up! But

I remember how I answered: red-faced,

I said, *Yes Sir, yes Sir,* I said.

15. 1960

Andrea Thomas

(Andrea, Speaker)

I wanted your hands on the tangle of my body,

cupping my breasts, my belly, my opening thighs

milky with desire, a whirlpool

you could drown in. I wanted the length

of your hard body pressing mine, imprinting

me forever on you, your arms and mine

twined securely as the roots of trees,

I wanted your mouth to taste my sex—

a banquet made ready for you only by gods.

I wanted your semen

to shatter the walls of my body,

Zeus to send thunderbolts, unbearable,

until I was limp. I wanted your sex

like a forbidden fruit: charged, opiate....

You thought I was a fallen angel,

or never was an angel, I, who offered

my cupped hands to you, held out my body

for your feast, for you to taste and drink,

to eat thereof. You thought desire stained me

like my monthly blood.

You wouldn't touch me to your lips—

you didn't want the howl of flesh

but something you could wind and stop,

that didn't cry, something you owned

and you could put into the ivory box

next to a braided ring of burnished hair.

I curse the House of Things, possession

that replaces love. I curse

the God of Eve who gave desire (lust,

you called it) and Mary, Immaculate,

who took it back. I feel

the unprimed cistern of my body

where a small trapped animal howls

in silence.

16. 1970

Venus Inebriate: Sarah Thomas Schwartz

(Andrea, speaker)

Naked she rose

out of her pond

in Connecticut

in slanted sunshine of late afternoon

big-breasted and deliberate

walked the pond's wall unsteadily

to the chair she sat in.

Aphrodite, too, sprang

from the water

from the sea at Paphos

foam-flecked and fair and free

watched by the gods

as she, by me

and little sons

who saw

but did not see.

17. 1975

Walls

(Andrea, speaker)

These broad stone walls have teeth of glass, jagged,

glinting, green; the moss is deep.

They capture brooks to make a pond

and waterfall. Two lichen-green arched bridges,

ferns rooted in their crevices, cross streams

where water stops to linger in small pools,

then eddies, high above the village—the road

was made for driving carriages and sleighs

to see the vista. *Calhoun* and *Chamberlain*

are carved, in 1843, in ledge,

that, treeless, guards the valley's view;

wintergreen and arbutus fight with moss

to share the meager soil that hunkers down

in hungry pockets of rejecting stone....

The fusty sleigh and carriage are now

a still life in the stable attic; the walls

have kept out traffic of the neighbors

and what it meant to, it kept in.

18. 1984

First Winter of Sarah Thomas Schwartz'

Unmarked Grave

(Andrea, speaker)

Spring rains were heavy when she died...

We pump the water, the back-hoe digger said,

but it fills and fills.

Impatient sons decided that they couldn't wait.

She won't care. Or know the difference!

Today I break a branch from a hawthorn tree

to write her name in drifted snow

in this New England town's first burial ground

where newest graves wear holly wreaths in season,

summer ferns and mosses choke the attempts of flowers,

and grey lichens strangle words carved into stone...

and I remember how we stood here, under umbrellas

and our own rain of tears; how I thought

only of how muddy, soiled, and soaked

would be her dress...of her mouth

so freshly dead, filling with water.

19. 1985

Photograph Album

(Andrea, speaker)

The album lies quite rigid, it defies my touch,

but I raise its leather cover that crumbles

into blackened dust, as though I disentomb a mummy.

The binding disintegrates to threads. Inside

the swaddled cover, gold dots squat

in hexagons, while flowers, petals stiff

as windmill arms, march into a maze

of framed rectangles filling every page.

Like a little prince and princess

John, Jr. and Moira posed before the camera:

in a ruched bonnet with satin bows, she holds

a rose in front of her white petticoats.

Sit still! don't move a finger!

Turn the page: they wear red capes

(they must be red, or blue) and corded cloches:

hers with a pom-pom, his with an ostrich feather.

Hold the pose! Put your hands together!

Their daddy promised to send photos

off to Mama (whom they can't remember)

far away in heaven. Turn the page:

Be quiet for Momma! A baby Persian lamb

encircles hats that frame their baby faces.

Don't fidget! sailor pleats, high-buckled shoes,

dressed for nursery tea... *Do you want Papa*

to see you messy! riding in the wicker pony cart.

The years march swiftly by inside the album...

Big silk roses sit atop

the pyramid of Moira's hat. Like her momma's

hair, hers twists, entwines along her neck.

John, Jr. is off to boarding school

in a suit of subtle plaid, a broad tie

flares under his wide white collar;

his eyes are sad...Did *he* break off the elephant's

proboscis, chip the coral piglets, corraled

on the piecrust table, next to me?

I turn the pages in the passing afternoon...

In a solarium in Hamptonwick-

upon-the-Thames, flowers stand white

and numb. There Moira sits, wrapped

in a cloud of tulle seeded with pearls

like stars that swirl around her satin dress.

From her floating hand a folded fan

with a silken tassel dangles.

                              Her father stands

beside her, in black knee-breeches and a cut-

away. Silver buttons march upwards

on his chest—a white "V" crisp

as a penguin's. He tucks a folded hat

in his gloved hand, on his left a silver sword hilt

rises; white stockings narrow calves

point to shoes with mirror buckles.

Both wait their moment to bow before

the Queen...glued there, in black and white.

Black-tasseled horses tramp through

this album from cover to disintegrating

cover. At last, John Williams, dressed in pearly

grey, arrested there, in bald profile,

in a lifelong wake for Jenny, facing him,

forever young, her eyes cast down,

her white curled ear like a bleached-out seashell,

white shoulders in her shroud

framed in dense black air.

                              Did her eyes open,

once, did she fix her unshielded gaze

on him, as she had never done in life,

and he recoil to clutch his severed heart,

ablaze and blinded?

I turn the page:

ivy turned to stone, climbs a marble cross.

It clings and curls. I close the album...

Now I hear the sound of girlish laughter

echo from the lawns, the splash of diving

louder than the waterfall...and I

turn back from insubstantial flesh—these shades—

to claim my warm and breathing daughters.

I call them, to come to the verandah,

sunlit now, I want to feel the touch

of them, their breath on mine. But first, I wash

the blackened powder from my hands.

20. 1990

They have flown away...

(Andrea, speaker)

Come with me, love of yesterday.

Sit beside me. We'll remember

how the wild geese glide, knowing

with a certainty their wings have lifted—

by now they've left their nesting place. We too

have been transported; from a different hill

we see deer silhouette against

the dusky sky, reddening with barberries

and maples' fire. All is still…

                                        Sit with me—

it is late—on these banks with greenest

laurel, by this errant stream: know

that underneath its absolutely

cold clear water, rainbows flash

like iridescent wings, the way the sunlight

slants through countless window panes,

when dust's little particles slide down

glistening wands of light.

                            Listen, there is

heat in light. And in reduction, space.

21. 1990

Flowers of Fire

(Andrea, speaker)

I led my daughters out of the circling dark

climbing into the blaze of day.

Still moving upwards they looked back

to where I'd stopped—on the edge of shadow,

half in sun—and waved. I see them yet,

I feel their brightness and it lights me.

Here, where the owl hoots at night

I hear my poor maimed one, who,

in darkness, dreams nightly of old wars,

shrieks with fresh wounds from new enemies,

still stiff with old wounds, not yet healed.

Across his remembered pond

he sees mist rising. He hears a waterfall.

The saber that visited the Queen is

now immobilized upon a different wall,

and there, too, hangs the portrait of Lord Cardigan,

saved from the auctioneer. On top the rolltop desk

the Silver and the Bronze Star rest, like gifts

from her who sprang, immaculate,

from a god's head, full-grown and fully armored—

Athena, who had no mother and would have

no sons...

       Between the metallic stars are photos

of three daughters, not in black and white:

they bloom, my flowers of fire!

They outshine flanking stars.